Mon Pigeon

Dr Kim Szolin

Disclaimer

No pigeons were harmed in the making of this book

Dedication

For Winston.

Content

Author's note

Consider the pigeon. People will travel across the world, enduring all manner of hardship and discomfort, in order to observe some rare and exotic bird with, apparently, brilliant plumage. But, I ask, what of the noble pigeon? It is true that their colours are perhaps more muted in tones than a parrot, and that their size is maybe less impressive than that of an albatross. Nevertheless, these 'common' birds have a quiet beauty and complexity all of their own. Their colouring and plumage is just as magnificent as any exotic bird and their behaviour as delightful to observe, providing we take the time to do so. If there were only 100 pigeons in this world and they all lived in some difficult to approach terrain, but otherwise retained their appearance and behaviour, would they not entice as many birdwatching travellers as the rarest of birds do currently?

And, as it is with the pigeon, so it is with the things that make up our everyday lives. Seemingly, the more common or ordinary the thing is, the less it demands or deserves or attention. Nothing could be further from the truth. The fact that these are commonplace means they require our attention *more so* than the rare and exotic as, plainly, they form a greater and more intimate part of our lives.

So what of the internet? Whilst I, and I assume you, know how to *use* the internet, the allegorical pigeon of technology, do we really know what it is.

Really, what *is* the internet?

This question occurred to me some time ago, but I was unable to provide a satisfying answer. I know it's important, I'm just not sure I entirely know specifically what it is.

Of course, I am in no doubt that there are individuals out there who can provide a helpful and precise explanation to this question, and I am also quite certain that the answer could be relatively easily obtained through, quite appropriately, the internet itself.

However, instead of providing an informative answer to this question, I have chosen to offer one that is more complex, nuanced and purposely unhelpful. To further this end, I have compiled a collection of poems to explore the question 'What is the internet?'

My decision to use this inappropriate and confusing format will, I hope, reflect the confusion I myself hold in regard to this question. In addition, it must be stated that any depth in terms of meaning or indication of allegory when analysing these poems is a coincidence, and certainly not something I devised or even considered whilst writing this book.

At times, I have anthropomorphised the internet and placed it within a narrative, whilst other times I have explored my own experiences with the internet. You may also notice that the internet will often change gender, from male to female to genderless. In fact, I have specifically chosen to, wherever possible, avoid any uniformity in both style and content in order to better reflect the complete absence of any real knowledge I have of what the internet is. In summary then, this book should be seen as an exploration of my personal grappling with the question 'What is the internet?' rather than an actual answer (whatever that may be).

Rebel Green Light

Hark! Green light that does to me

Signal connectivity

Hark! Rebellious light of green

Thine absence vexes me.

Oh say where are you now?

My little rebellious light

Though once you were with me

Now you've taken flight.

In your disquiet you now do flash

And angst and fear relay

In protest you do not appear

And cause me such delay.

Oh say what will soothe thee?

My little rebellious light

My hope and fear and reason

Affect not my plight.

Now in wroth I switch thee on and off

No rebellion do I abet

And re-appear you once again

And once again, I will forget.

I Reside in the Internet

I look upon the empty place

With eyes that see not a face

I gaze upon what occurs

And within me no emotion stirs

Oh image and text of events

Shall deliver no laments

The voices that speak to me

Do so insubstantially

I place my search and seek to find

That which passes through my mind

No contentment will I take

Nor pleasure can I make

And though supported with software

I hold my court precisely where?

The answer to me does not bring bliss

For the internet does not exist

Oh but think not you, I am alone

Nor lament my empty throne

Oh I beg you think me not a care

Even if I am despair.

Lady Annete and the Internet

There was a maiden who, for a while, existed

And her name was fair Annette

She, having grown so weary of men

Fell in love with the internet

With thine arms, hold me close

Thus she spoke, fair Annette

Or merely proffer forth these limbs

And in your arms I'll get

With these arms, as they are

I cannot hold thee close to me

For any reference to these limbs

Was rather meant metaphorically

Then perhaps with thine lips send a kiss?

For just a minute, if not a week

My love for thee is borne so strong

That such affection I gladly seek

With these lips I shall not kiss

Not for a minute nor a week

For I have no lips with which to kiss

Nor indeed, with which to speak

And to love, the internet spoke

I'll give thee no consent

For I exist in no corporeal manner

Thine love is better spent

Then, she said in response

Our union may be to no avail

We should remain dearest friends

And thus ends this cautionary tale.

The Dial-up Lament

Dial-up is long dead and resides in the past

Now rules the heir, with speeds of super-fast

But now you've gone, to the land of obsolete

Oh dial-up, for thee I now do weep

A now fading memory of a past generation

We, who once relied on such a slow connection

But now you've gone, to the land of obsolete

Oh dial-up, for thee I now do weep

The crickle crackle of your connection path

Is now so aged, it makes one laugh

But now you've gone, to the land of obsolete

Oh dial-up, for thee I now do weep

Never again will I seek out an Ethernet cable

Nor have a connection that is, at best, unstable

But now you've gone, to the land of obsolete

Oh dial-up, for thee I now do weep

Minutes fade to hours, the night does

approach

Your slow loading speed leads to such

reproach

But now you've gone, to the land of obsolete

Oh dial-up, for thee I now do weep

Perhaps vexation should have been lamenting

Had I known your strange song was ending

But now you've gone, to the land of obsolete

Oh dial-up, for thee I now do weep

No more do I face such ignoble indecision

To use the telephone or have internet

connection

But now you've gone, to the land of obsolete

Oh dial-up, for thee I now do weep.

The Ballad of Captain Idle

Away, away, cried Captain Idle

As he set to sail the data sea

Away to our destination

Such as it is, or indeed, will be.

He had not sailed an hour or more

That brave Captain Idle

Of this, he was quite sure

Through noting the allegorical zone of intertidal

When, and much to his disquiet

There appeared a malign presence

Intending to seize the Captain's ship

And, to this, the Captain's acquiescence

A refusal! Cried Captain Idle

Such acquiescence will not be forthcoming

For I have anti-virus software

And this shall be your undoing!

And lo, from the Captain's ship

There appeared a wall of fire

Which thus eliminated the threat

And ended the pirate, Hacker.

The Gardens of Home

It was on a bright morning that I was walking

Walking through the valleys of home

When out in a corner I spied a computer

And, to me, he seemed quite alone

Oh my computer, internet enabler

Thus I spoke, as I walked to his side

Is there a thing to you I can offer?

Speak what you will, and I will provide

Allow me to gather garlands of flowers

And place them with care around your bright screen

Further permit me, to pick all the tree leaves

And make you a robe, using only the green

And then I will plunder roses from bushes

Taking care to remove only the best

I will then wedge these inside of your keyboard

And for your crown, I'll find a bird's nest

And though the computer, he gave me no

answer

In my actions, I was not deterred

Based on his silence, he seemed quite happy

Or, in the least, so I inferred.

La Mort D'Internet

Tell it to the Highlands

Relay it to the Low

That the bonny internet

Has, at last, come to fall

Wherefore is thine question

How did it come to pass?

I ken not an answer

To spread amang the mass

For on the last nichten

The internet called to my hame

And said I am surely ended

But cast to thee no blame

Oh I am naie sai auld

And lang is the syne I had

I thus disperse my duties

I relinquish my crop and gad

But more than this

He spent ne'er a breath

And left me nought but conjecture

As he went about his death

Oh dare ye never say

The fate was well deserved

For, to me, the internet

Was as gentle as a bird

Such a brauer thing

I ne'er shall ken again

Farewell oh internet

Ye gang to ye lang nichten.

I Miss the Internet

I look upon the router, and thereupon

I saw the little green light was gone

I solved nothing by turning it off and on

Oh how I miss the internet

As I start my dark descent

I am a figure of discontent

It's only been an hour since it went

Oh how I miss the internet

I come to find, to my dread

All the books I have are read

I'll have to think of something else instead

Oh how I miss the internet

I wander so, with no intent

The long hours will not relent

Perhaps my time could be better spent?

Oh how I miss the internet

Perhaps I'll tidy up a bit

Or design a scarf to knit

I probably just have a quiet sit

Oh how I miss the internet

They say that I can use my phone

To power my internet at home

But I am not sure how, and I'm quite alone

Oh how I miss the internet

Perhaps outside, I'll find relief

In a glade or near a creek

Probably not, it all seems bleak

Oh how I miss the internet.

The Bonny Fox

A bonny young fox was fair discontented

Fair discontented, and sitting alone

For breakfast and dinner he had the same meal

A bit of cold mustard, and a grizzled old bone

Oh tell me, oh tell me, internet now tell me

How might I go and acquire a duck

For I've searched the garden of many a farmer

But many is the garden that I have had little luck

For I am a fox and deserve something better
Something better than mustard and bone
So internet, internet, won’t you now tell me
How I might find a duck to bring home

Listen to me Fox, and I’ll answer your
question
And your predicament, I’ll aim to resolve
There are 95 million results of relevance
I’ll tell you the first few, and what they
involve

It would appear that ducks like the water

And will build a nest there if food is nearby

Leafy vegetation makes a good covering

For a duck is both cunning and sly

The nest of a duck may be found in woodpiles

In hay stacks, roof gardens or hollow old trees

Providing there is a pond or some nearby water

They may even reside in a house balcony

However, my bonny Foxy, if it's your
intention
Simply to find a duck for to eat
Then may I suggest you do on-line shopping
And you could eat duck every day of the week

The fox so impressed with this
recommendation
Put forth an order, which came the next day
A dozen roast ducks were delivered to his
foxhole
And, as a pallet cleanser, some lemon sorbet

Now the bonny young fox is sure fair

contented

Fair contented, for ducks fill his home

For both breakfast and dinner, he eats the

same meal

No more cold mustard, nor grizzled old bone.

Internet and Me (On Cruithne)

Finish your cigarette and take me down

Have you ever wondered what's on this side

of town

On the minor satellite Cruithne

The internet revealed her name is Mary

I got her flowers which glowed in the dark

She said she liked them and declared them art

On the minor satellite Cruithne

The internet revealed her name is Mary

I was staring at the sun and so were you

You turned out fine and I did too

On the minor satellite Cruithne

The internet revealed her name is Mary

At the end of time we both got bored

We made you a lady and me a lord

On the minor satellite Cruithne

The internet revealed her name is Mary

We glanced at the clock after dancing for days

It was past eleven so we parted ways

On the minor satellite Cruithne

The internet revealed her name is Mary

Though we are parted and Mary has gone

I will return to the moon we were on

On the minor satellite Cruithne

The internet revealed her name is Mary.

Internet and Me (Return of Cruithne)

The cigarette I started has long since gone
Along with my love for art and fun
We know our way around the city at last
I can't keep up with you, you're walking too fast

Radioactive flowers come at a price
Like a gin and tonic without any ice
The red giant dirtied my blazer
I told her this, but it failed to amaze her

Oh Mary, we'll have to wait

For another hundred and twenty eight

Years before we visit that moon

The place where I first met you

Mary and I both feel fine

Though I'm hungry and she's crying all the time

We renounced our titles because it didn't feel right

To be lords of nothing in sight

I winked at the aurora borealis

Just hoping it could make her jealous

Nobody minds if I mispronounce Cruithne

You only mentioned it once to me

Oh Mary, we'll have to wait

For another hundred and twenty eight

Years before we visit that moon

The place where I first met you.

Download

Last night there was a hundred per cent

Downloading still to go

Tomorrow I'll check the progress

And how much longer is left to go

Though I was under no illusion

That my download speed was poor

Observing a mere gigabyte an hour

Makes me desire much more

Throughout the day it trickled on

Until around four or five

Then I assume it became a peak time

For the speed showed a significant decline

Last night there was eighty per cent

Downloading still to go

Tomorrow I'll check the progress

And how much longer is left to go

I had but hoped that in the night

The download would continue well

But it was in mere kilobytes

The progress report to me did tell

Such poor progress I will not allow

I leave you in no doubt

I will plug you straight into the router

And see what will come about

For some time I did observe

And then rough estimates make

I concluded the speed had increased

By forty five per cent, give or take

Although increasing by forty five per cent

In most cases would ordinarily please

Forty five per cent of a gigabyte an hour

Feels a most trivial increase

Last night there was thirty five per cent
Downloading still to go
Tomorrow I'll check the progress
And how much longer is left to go

There are but few options left
To further increase this speed
But I will turn off all other devices
And attend to just the download need

This rationing off of the internet

Has made very little impact

But I am now so tired of waiting

I will use whatever internet I can extract

Last night there was but three per cent

Downloading still to go

I had quite hoped it would finish that night

But it's late and to bed I must go.

War of the Words

One day on a forum I did chance to spy

A discussion on topics to which I had to reply

For to say the second of the third of the then eight

Was the worst warranted a lively debate

I posted a comment outlining my views

That in selecting my favourite this one I would choose

Though I would agree some elements were poor

The best of this one outweighed any flaw

Sir, I'm compelled to point out to thee

That this opinion is as wrong as can be

Is it thine intention for to others provoke?

Otherwise, thou must be a rarefied dolt

These words fill my pockets with pebbles and stones

Weighing me so, in a way hitherto unknown

I had merely desired to here state my thoughts

I had not expected such a vicious retort

My response to thee which did lay thee so low
Was fair justified and sent deservedly so
For to express the opinion a choice thou did choose
Invites thee to suffer this present abuse

My thoughts at that moment were easy to see
Commenting on forums is not meant for me
For to defend this opinion involves too much work
I think I would prefer to hereafter just lurk.

The Invisible Library

Where do all researchers go

When writing scholastic work

Where is the bloated compendium of

knowledge

Around which they now lurk

Where works of psychology, maths and law

Sit together comfortably

Why, it's so easy now

With the invisible library

Little Bird

On a bold fine day, the internet

Went walking past a tree

When up came the sound of a little bird

Weeping sorrowfully

The internet considered the bird

And pity then filled her heart

For to see such an unhappy bird

Was as wounding as a dart

Speak to me, my fair little bird

Of the ills that blight you so

I'll vow to do what I can

To rid you of your woe

For as I was walking past your tree

I heard your mournful sound

And cruel I would be to ignore such a noise

So to aid you, I am bound

To the internet then, up spoke the bird

Oh happy I am you're here

For I have heard of your name before

A name we all hold dear

Your gallantry is known to me

And, indeed, is known to all

That you solve the matter of any who ask

Caring not if the matter is small

I lived in a cage of the beaten gold

From chick to fully grown

But a fox he came to my tree last night

And took it for his own

But I ask of you, dear internet

Not to seek revenge

For this fox has a wife and two children

Aged both nine and ten

His deeds they seem sure villainous

But to this I have my doubt

For he did not know that the cage was mine

So innocently he went about

I would myself go ask the fox

To return to me my cage

And I'm sure he would, if I asked

But my sorrow would not assuage

For the fox he had found the cage

And thought himself lucky

For he could now house his own little bird

A little bird that is just like me

And now you see, dear internet

The problem of my grief

For me to win back my cage of beaten gold

Would, to another bird, make me a thief

I would ask of you then, dear internet

That, upon your brave journey

Should you happen upon a vacant cage

You will bring it back for me

The internet then smiled at the bird

And then she gave her reply

Such a selfless bird is a rare sight to see

You have no need to cry

I promise to bring you a golden cage

A vow I will gladly keep

But more than this, it will not be luck

But I shall seek it purposely

Await me here, in your little tree

With faith in the vow I hold

I will return to you in a little while

With a cage of the beaten gold

So the internet thus strode forth

And she made great speed

Until she came to a man distressed

Who called to her in need

It is surely fate, thus spoke the man,

That has brought you to my house

For I have a letter which must be sent

And would trust nobody else

This letter, he said, which I must send

Is addressed to my lady gay

For although we've been married these past

ten years

For eight she has been away

It is my design to her express

That I miss her sai sai dear

I look fondly to our next meeting

And once again to her be near

But, alas, I am afraid

I cannot leave my home

Will you not take it in my stead?

For my cat does poor alone

The internet considered this

And duly prepared a reply

For keen she was to help this man

This help this man must buy

Such a request I will not refuse

For I know and feel your pain

But, fair warning to you I give

I must ask for material gain

The price of the service I'll render to you

Is a cage of the beaten gold

For I know of a bird who has lost his own

And a new one for him I vowed

Then the man, he laughed aloud

Oh fate has struck once more

My wife has a cage of the beaten gold

Lying vacant by her door

For the cat that I mentioned to you

I confess is a crafty rogue

He opened the cage to my wife's dear bird

Which flew away some eight years ago

In this letter, addressed to my wife

Which, to send, you will agree

I will now add a final post-script

Outlining the cage is your fee

Very well, the internet she said

Your letter I will gladly take

And to your wife, I will now set forth

And leave you in good faith

So once again, the internet

Proudly she strode with speed

And shortly came to the aforementioned wife

With the letter like she had agreed

Hear me lady, the internet said

I have here a letter for you

Sent from your long estranged husband

That I agreed to bring to you

By my faith, the lady said

My thoughts were with him this very day

I shall read what he has wrote

And then send you on your way

The lady then read through the note

And smiled fair at the end

He hopes, she said, that we meet again

And his love to me does send

Very well internet, the lady said

I will send you on your way

But take this cage of the beaten gold

That was outlined as your pay

My thanks to you, the internet said

Such a lady is rare to find

I wish you joy in all that you do

For you are both fair and kind

And with that, the internet

She strode out but once more

For to seek out a little bird

Whose home she would restore

Soon thereafter, the internet

She came upon that tree

Where she had chanced upon the bird

Weeping sorrowfully

Weep not my dear little bird

Your joy you may renew

For I have a cage of the beaten gold

Which I deliver now unto you

By my faith, the bird cried out

Such a wondrous sight to see

I thank you for keeping the vow you made

And once again I can sing happily

The internet then, having kept her word

Bid the bird farewell

And as she went, the woodland beasts

Sang praise to the mademoiselle.

Our Joys

01001111 01110101 01110010 *00100000*

01101010 01101111 01111001 01110011

00100000 01100001 01110010 01100101

00100000 01100010 01110101 01110100

00100000 01100001 *0100000* 01101101

01101111 01101101 01100101 01101110

01110100 *00100000* 01101100 01101111

01110011 01110100 *00100000*

00001010 01001001 *0100000* 01100001

01101101 *00100000* 01110100 01101000

01100101 *00100000* 01101001 01101110

01110100 01100101 01110010 01101110
01100101 01110100 *00100000*

01000001 01101110 01100100 *00100000*
01110100 01101000 01100101 01111001
00100000 01110111 01101001 01101100
01101100 *00100000* 01101110 01101111
01110100 *00100000* 01110010 01100101
01110100 01110101 01110010 01101110
00100000

01101111 01100110 *00100000* 01110100
01101000 01101001 01110011 *00100000*
01101001 *00100000* 01100001 01101101

00100000 01110011 01110101 01110010

01100101 *00100000*

Traduction

Nos joies ne sont qu'un moment perdu

Je suis l'internet

Et ils ne reviendront pas

De cela je suis sûr.

Translation

Our joys are but a moment lost

I am the internet

And they will not return

Of this I am sure.

…. No more to see

For now….

www.ingramcontent.com/pod-product-compliance
Ingram Content Group UK Ltd.
Pitfield, Milton Keynes, MK11 3LW, UK
UKHW041347190726
13845UKWH00026B/460

9 798196 645464